About the Author

My life has been eventful and traumatic which has left me battling many demons inside my head.

I was once told by a therapist to write down my feelings, over the years and tears my words turned into poems and it became therapeutic and healing.

Although I take pride in my appearance and being healthy, the main reason I go to the gym daily is for my mental wellbeing and the release of negative emotions.

Unfortunately I broke my leg in an unforeseen accident and my independence had gone and not being able to exercise had a negative impact on me and I didn't expect the mental battle that I faced.

I had no choice but to board an unhinged emotional roller coaster. I picked the pen and paper up again and poured my heart out to the pages. I opened all the tightly locked boxes in my head and expressed pain, joy and giggles through my words.

My poems are about my real life experiences and touch upon some heavy and current topics that the world is dealing with at present.

Ultimately I hope my poems touch or help someone in need.

Poetry

Em Luis

Poetry

Vanguard Press

A CIP catalogue record for this title is
available from the British Library.

ISBN 978 1 80016 672 1

*Vanguard Press is an imprint of
Pegasus Elliot Mackenzie Publishers Ltd.*
www.pegasuspublishers.com

First Published in 2024

**Vanguard Press
Sheraton House Castle Park
Cambridge England**

Printed & Bound in Great Britain

Dedication

To my dad, Joao Nelson Luis and Pops.

Acknowledgements

Thank you to my beautiful children Lui and Honey. The centre of my world, who showed me true love. They brought out my inner lioness. They gave me purpose and grounded me. They don't realise they saved me. I'm so immensely proud of the young adults they're becoming.

To G. Where do I start?

He's my biggest cheerleader and my partner in crime. He provides endless love and support. No matter what life throws at me, I know I will never have to deal with it alone.

Liam, who taught me so much about myself. Exposed me to experiences so I could realise how strong I actually am.

Last but not least, Mr. Pink, my OG chihuahua. He blessed me with over sixteen years of his life. By my side through the good, bad and ugly. The most loyal soul and kindest dog.

The Key

Everybody has one,
So powerful and unique,
Many don't know how to use it,
But it's the truth that we seek,

Conditioned since young,
Programmed to abide,
It's what they want us to be,
The truth that they hide,

But the truth that we follow,
Lies deep within,
Buried inside us,
Underneath the skin,

Beneath the surface
And into the soul,
It's where you're find it,
It's your life long goal,

If only they told us,
When we were young,
That we are the creator,
A beauty unsung,

We have the key,
To the box unopened,

We are in control,
But this is unspoken,

So if I can teach you,
Let me tell you one thing,
You are your own reason,
In the universe, you are king,

A simple requirement,
Is to believe,
Really feel it inside,
And the fruits you will receive,

All it takes is one thought,
Believe, it will manifest,
Chill the soul,
The universe will do the rest,

Don't believe what they told you,
The truth is only yours,
Subconscious is the key,
It will open all the doors

Poem About My Poems

I had a lot of trauma,
Surrounding my younger years,
The hardship and pain,
Continuously interferes,

So many therapists and docs,
Tried so hard to understand,
They tried their best to fix me,
But it was all my hands,

"Write down your feelings"
I was once told,
I put pen to paper
And my poems would unfold,

Through the art of writing,
I'd unleash my feelings,
I'd let the pain go
And begin the healing,

Life was never meant to be easy,
The years brought more pain,
I fought on even harder,
And poems I would maintain,

So in my dark times,
I could always shed some light,
Even though I was hurting,
I was ready for the fight,

I found a way to express myself,
A way I could let anger go
In a non-self-destructive way,
A way that made my talent show,

It's kind of like self-therapy,
A place where my mind does ease,
I escape from reality,
Lost in words, I appease.

Story Teller

Your story doesn't always begin happy,
Doesn't make you who you are,
Some of us didn't have choices,
When we think back that far,

The cards we were dealt,
From such a tender age,
Forced to play the hand,
Many left in rage,

When we finally realise,
It's our book and our pen,
We can write a new chapter,
We can actually start again,

A task that seems so simple,
It's harder than it looks,
It involves self-healing,
Many self-help books,

You will be left questioning,
Who you really are,
A lot of persistent, self-talk,
Will only take you so far,

You are not your past,
It no longer exists,
Be present and mindful,
Though your mind resists,

Through hard work,
Dedication and will,
You will have a breakthrough,
Dictating your mind is your skill,

You will take on each day,
With your blank page to write,
The best story teller,
Undoubtedly will be you tonight.

Motivation

Before you get out of bed,
And prepare to start your day,
Self-doubt begins to loom,
Don't let it ruin your day,

Realise you're your own cheerleader,
And it's your chant to sing
Sing your chant loud,
And virtues it will bring,

The power that you have,
Is yours and yours alone,
Though you may doubt yourself,
Just look how much you have grown,

Life is far too short,
Go harder than yesterday,
Push past your comfort zone,
And you will see brighter days,

The hard days will present themselves,
It's a challenge we must accept,
Put your fighting gear on,
And remember the promise you kept,

Tell yourself you have got this,
You are a fighter, you are strong,
You will not be defeated,
A happy life is where you belong.

Higher Energy

Higher self or universe,
It is there we must admit,
The source of energy,
The frequency we transmit,

We all give off vibrations,
Whilst we live in our human suits,
Navigating our way,
In our thoughts we recruit,

Thoughts become things,
Feelings create our reality,
We are in control,
Of the energy's formality,

We do not live in a 3D world,
This is all an illusion,
The frequency we vibrate,
Is our biggest solution,

The power is inside us,
The key is in our hand,
Raising our vibration,
Is what we need to understand,

The power of our thoughts,
Should be our main concern,
Feeding them with positivity,
And positivity will return,

Our minds are incredible,
The subconscious doesn't know fact,
So whatever we tell it,
On our lives it will impact,

It's time to let go,
Of the emotions holding us back,
Believe we are warriors of light,
Step away from the cloud of black,

If we all believed this concept,
Our lives would surely change,
Our frequency is raised,
And our vibration rearranged,

The ability of an egregore,
Shows us the power of the mind,
If we all come together,
Energy intertwined,

We would be unstoppable,
To vibrate all as one,
A massive forcefield,
Like the Earth begun.

Recovery

Recovery
I want to tell you my journey,
A story of darkness and pain,
Something I'm over coming,
to see the sun through the rain,

Anyone who knows me,
Knows I can't sit still,
Anyone who knows me,
Knows the gym is my anti-depressant pill,

Standing in a country,
Ready for my op,
Excited, scared and lonely,
And all of a sudden I drop,

Woken to fear,
Rushing through my veins,
How did I end up on the floor?
And why am I in so much pain?

Little did I know,
My story had just begun,
Fighting back the tears,
The news I heard made me numb,

Broken leg and ankle, they told me,

Probably not a biggie to you,
But my independence was taken
There was nothing I could do,

The pain is intense
And the recovery is long,
But I'm a little fighter
And have no choice but to be strong,

My demons came to haunt
As they always do,
No gym that could save me,
I couldn't see a way through,

The black cloud got the better of me,
And darkness was by my side,
I knew it wouldn't be easy,
I was in for a bumpy ride,

Found the strength inside me,
To realise I am more,
More than the pain,
Preventing me from putting my leg upon the floor,

So I work on myself daily,
The struggle is still so real,
I won't let it get the better of me,
Because I am the real deal,

So if you're suffering in silence,
Please know you are never alone,
Everybody is fighting a battle,
Inside the body they call home

My Medicine

A building you are,
But to me you are much more,
The treasures you hold,
Behind your front door,

You are my medicine,
Endorphins you release,
I put in the effort,
And let the happiness increase,

I don't always feel like going,
Some days I feel like driving by,
But I won't see the results,
Unless I'm willing to try,

Leg day I dread,
After pain is surreal,
I do it to look good,
But more about how I feel,

So pick up a weight,
And feel the burn,
De-stress your mind,
And happiness you will earn.

Empaths

Empathy is a superpower,
Or so I've been told,
We absorb others' emotions,
Which we cannot control,

It can be overwhelming,
Stuck in your emotions,
Fighting your battles,
Replying with devotion,

We are very highly tuned,
Our senses are always on alert,
We are happy to help,
But the ones left feeling hurt,

When we get our gut feeling,
Believe we are true,
It's us trying to save you,
Through our clearer view,

We have huge hearts,
A very unique view,
This isn't always easy,
As our own happiness we pursue,

Beware, kind empaths,
When you start your day,
The energy vampires,
You will have to slay,

They drain us slowly,
Fill up on our kind,
Leaving us empty,
While they feel better in mind,

This is when,
We have to step back,
Return to nature,
And our feelings we unpack,

Digest the day,
Put yourself back together,
An empath's survival tactics,
Are ever so clever,

We have been put on this earth,
Our job is to heal,
Embrace it, empaths,
Your superpower is real.

Addiction

Your judged for caring,
But all you want is to support,
No one to help,
Your left feeling distraught,

It's not your addiction,
But it might as well be,
There's no end in sight,
This is abuse in some degree,

Endless excuses,
But I know who you are,
I'm on your side,
But you're pushing to far,

Gone past the point,
Of me enabling,
Backed in a corner,
Your power is disabling,

Please stop your lies,
I can't take much more,
You're bleeding me dry,
I'm heading for the door,

Who's the stranger?
Where is the man I used to know?
You're in disguise,
Let your true self show,

My help is unwanted,
This is your battle to fight,
Unwilling I step back,
This is your story to write,

Make your words happy,
Full of love and joy,
Please start writing now,
Or your drug will destroy

Food Demon

This is not how I wanted to start,
But I don't see any other way,
To try to explain this disease,
I have no choice but to say,

It's more than the food,
It's all about control,
Starving or binging,
It eats into your soul,

It consumes the mind,
And takes over each day,
Avoiding or overeating,
It becomes the only way,

To the outsider,
We are insane,
Obsessing over calories,
But this is all to maintain,

The distorted image,
That we believe is true,
The reflection in the mirror,
The image we wish to pursue,

It's always out of reach,
It's always too far away,
But the inner eating demon,
Will guide us through the day,

Restricting or overeating,
The discipline is installed,
The cycle begins again,
Friends and family left appalled,

Food is not the enemy,
It' wants us to survive,
Fighting the food demon,
It's the only way to stay alive.

Was I That Bad?

At sixteen, I was still a baby,
When you showed me the door,
I couldn't quite believe what was happening,
Am I not worth anything more?

Your actions sent me to spiral,
No guidance but my own,
Just me, myself and I,
I had no place to call home,

Pretending that I didn't care,
Of course, was all just a lie,
Put a face on in public,
All alone I would cry,

I knew I was different,
From the other three,
Stubborn character I was,
That I would not disagree,

Crying out for help,
Was all I was trying to do,
But you didn't get this,
You didn't have a clue,

So at sixteen I became an adult,
This was never my choice,
It was put on me so suddenly,
I didn't have a voice,

Was your life easier?
Now that I was gone,
Are you happy now?
Did I ever really belong?

These were the questions
 I asked my teenage years,
I still don't know the answers,
Forever not knowing it appears.

Green-Eyed Monster

You only see a shell,
And it's my shell to create
Why does my appearance,
Leave you full of hate?

You're entitled to your opinion,
That is everybody's right,
But why be so spiteful?
Why not be polite?

The real reason is,
It lies before my eyes,
Though you try to fool me,
Green-eyed monster in disguise,

You envy is apparent,
It oozes through your pores,
It makes you really ugly,
Which I find hard to ignore,

I'm the bigger person,
Vileness that you are,
Your comments don't affect me,
Which you find bizarre,

You need educating,
To expand your small mind,
You're only hurting you,
When you are so unkind,

Your jealousy doesn't affect me,
It only affects you,
Doesn't the sound pathetic,
Your tactics you should review

Suicide

The aftermath of suicide,
Leaves a crippling effect,
Questioning continuously,
What led you into this wreck?

Self-guilt begins to rise,
Inner blame runs free,
What could I have done better?
How could I make you see?

That this is not the answer,
It doesn't have to end,
I can help you get over this,
I've got your back, I'm your friend,

My words weren't enough,
My support pushed away,
You didn't want my help,
You didn't want to see another day,

As painful as it was,
It was your decision to make,
To end your life so suddenly,
This was your biggest mistake,

But now your pain was gone,
Mine began to grow,
Suicide grief is far different,
Your loss let that show,

Many years of pain,
Built up anger and hurt,
Frustration and tears,
All my feelings would divert,

How did I let this happen?
Am I really to blame?
Overwhelmed with emotions,
I hang my head in shame,

The pain is always there,
I believe it will never go,
I've had to learn to live with it,
Many self-talks I undergo,

This is what you wanted,
You wanted to be free,
You are safe and happy now,
And you are watching over me.

Men's Mental Health

It's the silent killer,
That stalks the boys and men,
Reaping havoc within them,
A broken record again,

We need to be more open,
The issue is bigger than us,
Men's mental health is troubling,
We all need to discuss,

Suicide rates,
Have hit an all-time high,
Why are they suffering?
Boys, it's okay to cry,

It doesn't make you weak,
You need to talk,
Just take your time,
Don't run before you can walk,

Be more open,
There's no need to be scared,
We are not here to judge,
Just show you, you're cared,

Your feelings are precious,
Don't worry, I will take your hand,
Guide you through the darkness,
And on to your promised land,

Don't fear, you are not alone,
I'm right by your side,
We will do this together,
It's all in your stride,

And all of a sudden
You are finally there,
You made it through the darkness,
Your light we both share.

Trolls

Your weapon of choice is a keyboard,
You never turn up to the battlefield,
Stuck behind your screen,
With your vicious fingers you yield,

Typing out your hatred,
Is your number one skill,
Full venom inside you,
Your life must be so fulfilled,

Your vile words don't hurt me,
For I grew thick skin,
I am talking for the others,
Their voice is where I will begin,

Were you bullied at school?
Or did you get beaten by your mum?
Were you always rejected?
Is that why trolling is fun?

There must be evil inside you,
That's why you act this way,
Your blood must run black,
With the appalling actions you display,

But horrid little troll,
This doesn't give you the right,
To bully innocent people,
To shed darkness on their light,

Take a look in the mirror,
Because that's where it began,
Do you like your troll reflection?
Was that always your plan?

All that energy you put in,
Trying to ruin people's days,
Concentrate on yourself,
And learn that kindness is the only way

Liam

Before I gave up on you,
Please know I gave it my all,
So many parts broken,
My back pressed against the wall,

You pushed me too far
Yet I held on so tight
I wanted to save you
I was ready to help you fight,

Poisoning your body slowly
It took hold you, like nothing I've seen before
More powerful than I'll ever be,
Me begging you, knees pressed against floor,

Nothing I could do to stop it,
Defeated, I had to let you see
Your choice was so painful
Selfish and raw

Confused and broken, I couldn't take much more,
Years past and now I understand why
Why you could no longer be here,
It was your time for the sky,

So thank you for the lessons you taught me,
Stronger and wiser I've become
Never forgetting the memories
Head held high to the sun

Fly High

I knew the day would come,
At some point you would leave,
But nothing would prepare me,
My baby, I still wanted to believe,

I brought you up to be independent,
To always stand on your two feet,
To take on every challenge,
And never accept defeat,

Though you are still so young,
And have lots of lessons to learn,
I had to let you fly the nest,
Much to my concern,

The bubble wrap I wrapped you in,
You popped one by one,
You no longer needed it,
Grown man but always my son,

All the lessons I taught you,
You listened and took in,
You showed me through your actions,
That you were ready to begin,

You spread your wings open,
And took your first flight,
I've never felt so lost,
You have never felt so right,

This wasn't about me,
This is all about you,
Fly high, my baby boy,
May all your dreams come true.

Lui

I was eighteen when you were handed to me
Back in 2002,
Young, scared and unsure
Or what I was supposed to do,

But you stared at me
With your big green eyes,
The lioness kicked in,
And I soon realised,

That you were my reason,
I had to believe,
That anything was possible,
With my cub we would achieve,

We grew strong together
Showed the world what we were about,
An unbreakable bond,
That no one could doubt,

No longer stands beside me,
My little cub
Now before me a fierce full-grown lion,
Full of love

No words can describe,
How proud I really am,
How blessed and lucky
To have my very own superman.

You Are Never Alone

My job is to protect you,
To keep you safe and warm,
Shield you from the darkness,
And watch my cub transform,

There's nothing that I wouldn't do,
I'd go to the end of the Earth and back,
To see you smile,
To keep you on track,

Life was so simple,
Before your demons came,
I felt so helpless,
Was I to blame?

Watching you struggle,
Tore me apart,
Distraught and powerless,
A constant pain in my heart,

No support from loved ones,
They didn't have a clue,
I was better off without them,
It was just me and you,

So I took your hand,
And we walk side by side,
I will never leave you,
I will always be your guide,

The daily battle you face,
I'm your soldier, I'm next to you,
Lioness and cub,
We will make it through,

If I could have just one wish,
I'd take all your pain,
I'd release your demons,
And happiness you would gain,

You are much bigger and more powerful,
Then you realise yet,
In time you will see,
That you are the bigger threat,

Until that time has come,
In the shadows I will stand,
Waiting for your call,
Waiting for you to reach for my hand.

Scars

Each has a story,
Some I'm not willing to tell,
Some are further than skin deep,
And pushed me to the borders of hell,

It took some time,
For me to be comfortable with them on my skin,
It took longer,
For the ones within,

They are proof of my battle,
And how versatile I've become,
I've been knocked down a few times,
Trained myself to become numb,

I try find beauty within them,
Because they are part of my life story,
I succeeded on the battlefield,
It's my time for glory,

Gone are the times,
For me to be so judgmental of my human suit,
The scars make me who I am,
This I could not dispute,

If I obtain more,
On my journey that's not yet done,
Another battle faced,
Another battle won,

I will wear them with pride,
And let my victory show,
I am a light warrior,
After every battle I grow.

Recovery Part 2

It's been two months,
Since my leg and ankle broke,
Nine weeks of an emotional roller coaster,
So many unwanted thoughts I'd provoke,

Many tears I cried,
Most hours spent alone,
Questioning who I am,
How can I feel this low about a broken bone?

So active but so restricted,
The frustration began to build,
I've been through a lot worse,
In self-help I'm skilled,

I had to dig deeper,
There must be a reason why,
I found myself in this situation,
And there was no need to cry,

"Be still," said the universe,
I had no choice but to comply,
Did your command have to be so severe?
I'm still yet to get a reply,

The answer I want,
Lies solely with me,
I'm still on the journey,
I think the universe would agree,

I've grown as a person,
In numerous ways,
My growth continues,
As I enter the next phase.

Postnatal Depression

Nine months you wait,
For your bundle of joy to arrive,
Nobody tells you,
PND will leave you clutching to survive,

Confused by these unwanted feelings,
Longing for that instant bond,
I don't feel normal,
Emotions far and beyond,

In different shapes and forms,
You present yourself in so many ways,
So many women affected,
All praying it's a phase,

You shame us in public,
We want to be the same,
As the mother's in the park,
To them, it's fun and games,

You are a good mother,
PND, I'm not ready to surrender,
You won't take my bond,
I'm the judge, you're the offender

Narcissist

Your grandiose of self-importance,
Makes one stand back,
Dumbfounded and amazed,
How you're constantly on attack,

Your level of arrogance,
Is on another scale,
Whilst you try to imitate,
Nothing but a narcissistic male,

You twist every conversation,
Just to benefit your needs,
Make us feel unworthy,
In your game to succeed,

You exploit us with guilt,
Feeling no shame at all,
Dust your shoulders off, narcissist,
You have made us feel very small,

Your constant need for praise,
I find quite sad,
Longing for admiration,
Is that why you are so mad?

Your sense of entitlement,
Is so extreme,
Lengths you're willing to go,
To ruin someone's self-esteem,

To frequently demean,
Must be your get-up and go,
Belittling and bully,
Is the narcissist's show,

It took some time,
Before I removed,
The rose-tinted glasses,
Of which you disapproved,

But that was only because,
I could finally see,
Who you really are,
Narcissist guarantee,

Abuse

You stand in the doorway,
Your height towers over me,
Anger is your answer,
I dare not disagree,

Your eyes drain of colour,
Your veins on full display,
Your spitting venom at me,
There's no point trying to convey,

I'm not trying to fight you,
I want you to calm down,
Take a moment to breathe,
Rest your face, stop the frown,

But this would only anger you,
And make it worse for me,
So I shut my mouth and prepare myself,
For what it's going to be,

You take me by the throat,
And lift me off the ground,
My body is trembling,
Your shouting, I don't hear a sound,

Everything is in slow motion,
As you launch me through the air,
I wish time would hurry up,
I wish I was anywhere but there,

The remorse that you feel,
Is always too little too late,
Cradling me like a baby
When you put me in this state,

I forgave you every time,
I was far too weak to see,
That it was you in the wrong,
You were abusing me.

Seizures

You creep up on me,
Like a stranger in the night,
Possess my body,
Anxiety reaches its height,

You have full control
You fill my body full of fear,
I can't escape,
Wishing you would disappear.

Your cruel intentions,
Leave me drained,
Question who I am,
Your forces have me chained.

Wearing your evilness,
Though it's only a short time,
I don't know who I am,
I'm left with a mountain to climb,

A mountain full of confusion,
I mountain full of dismay,
I take a deep breath,
I've got this, I will keep you at bay,

Though your presences,
I can still feel,
You are no more than a seizure,
And I'm willing to heal

Daddy

You were taken so quickly,
No time for goodbyes,
Ever so young,
But not too young to realise

Lost and broken,
Life will never be the same,
Now that you had gone,
I felt I had little to gain,

With such heavy news,
My knowledge was slight,
But far from confused,
My daddy was out of sight,

Overwhelmed with emotions,
Uprooted and taken,
Many tears I've shed,
Body left shaken,

No time to think,
Overnight my childhood disappeared,
Had to grow up quickly,
As much as I feared,

Listening to mum,
Cry herself to sleep,

Tried to block it out,
But it would forever creep,

Had to face the fact,
That you were gone,
I couldn't see you no more,
But in my heart, you belong,

And Daddy,
That's where you will forever stay,
Until we meet again
Until that day

Girls

Do you ever stop and think,
What it's like for us,
Or is this what it has come to?
Girls you must be robust,

We are not asking for a lot,
Just to live and enjoy,
Have a night out
Without your mission to destroy,

We are told to cover our drinks,
And always watch our back,
Always be aware,
In case of an attack,

I will take the stand,
On behalf of us all,
We don't live in the cave ages,
In men, shivery we must install,

To be intoxicated,
To walk the streets alone,
The feeling of secrecy,
To always make it home,

To never have to worry,
What your intentions are,
To be able to flirt,
Without you taking it too far

Patience

Not blessed with patience,
A thing I had to learn,
The waiting game,
When is it my turn?

The lesson of tolerance,
Is a hard pill to take,
Not accepting delay,
Was a mistake I would make
,
I wanted to speed up time,
I wanted it yesterday,
But I had to be mindful,
For this is the only way,

Advancing new ideas,
Ready to get things done,
Always in a hurry,
Even before it's begun,

The bearing of annoyance,
Self-taught along the way,
An ability of willingness,
Is how I start the day,

Suppress the misfortune,
Endurance of provocation
Compose my mind,
This is not aggravation,

So I remain calm,
It will be here when is ready,
Mindful of the moment,
My pace is now steady.

Dancing for Dollars

You walk into the club, it's your space,
You have arrived
Little do you know,
I'm about to take you for a ride,

The experience will thrill
The entertainment is on point,
I do my best to please
Try never to disappoint,

Centre stage I take,
I come into my own
My two songs prepared
The pole becomes my home,

Your eyes fixate
You're like putty in my hand
All I want is your wallet,
I hope you understand,

So I sit on next beside you
Plying you with drink,
Conversation bores me
But your money makes me rethink,

So I stay a little longer
Listen to bull
All the while you're wasted
And my pockets become full,

Drink has taken over
Now you're hoping for a grope
Don't put your hands upon me
Darling, I sell hope.

Australia

At the young age of sixteen,
Kicked out and nowhere to go,
I got an invitation,
Australia down below,

Too good of an offer,
I surely couldn't decline,
So I packed my huge backpack,
And headed for the sunshine,

I landed in Perth,
That's where my adventure began,
We were going to cross Oz,
In a VW camper van,

The experience was unreal,
At such a young age,
Surrounded by older people,
I felt I was on a different page,

I saw this as an opportunity,
I could learn and grow,
So I took in everything Oz had to offer,
And the gains began to show,

By the time I got to Sydney,
The money had nearly run out,
Time to get a job,
But working visa I was without,

That's where dancing for dollars,
Began to unfold for me,
Couldn't believe how much I could earn,
I felt so liberated and free,

My new job kept us out there,
For an extra twelve weeks,
But I knew I had to go home soon,
I was counting down the sleeps,

Australia, you taught me so much,
Memories I will never forget,
I've been back three times since,
And I will be back more times yet.

G.

Cliché you may say,
But I wasn't looking when I found you,
Didn't know if I was ready,
There you were, a bolt out of the blue,

I couldn't help myself falling,
Tried to hold back with all my might,
I let myself go,
Falling in love was my birth right,

But the situation was dawning,
They were going to take you away,
I knew I was going to lose you,
I was counting down the days,

This time was different,
I didn't want to run a mile,
This time was different,
I wanted to walk down the aisle,

I stayed true to my word,
And stuck by your side,
Head full of doubts,
Heart full of pride,

Time spent away,
Felt ever so lonely,
Challenged most days,
The reason my one and only,

We did it together,
We made it through,
I trusted my heart,
Deep inside I knew,

Years gone by,
We stand strong together,
An unstoppable bond,
That is made to last forever.

Soulmate

The connection is instant,
Feels like this being has been in your presence before,
Their aura is warming,
Their personality you need to explore,

Faced with their beauty,
That shines from within,
Enchanted conversation,
Thinking where have they been?

When your paths finally cross,
And the connection is met,
There's nothing quite like it,
A day you will never forget,

This person sees you,
For whom you really are,
All your faults and flaws,
And still, you are their guiding star,

Not an ounce of judgement,
You are perfect to them,
As they are to you,
Two rosebuds on a stem,

You grow together,
Together you become strong,
You can't believe this is happening,
The feeling you have yearned for so long,

Up until now,
You thought a soulmate was a myth,
A fantasy mate,
Not someone you need to spend your life with,

Here they are,
A beacon of light,
Two souls connected,
Two flames enlight,

You are bonded for eternity,
Infinity and beyond,
Your frequency is met,
Surrendering yourself to the soulmate bond.

Covid

It affected us all,
Invading us in so many ways,
We became prisoners,
What we believed to be days,

The days became months
We were all trapped inside,
Climbing the walls,
So many rules applied,

Each of us all,
Will have a lockdown story to tell,
Some really enjoyed it,
For others it was hell,

No one had a clue,
At least we were all in it together,
Groundhog Day,
Was lasting forever,

A baby boom
Rise in divorce,
Families under pressure,
Covid is the driving force,

It was a first,
We did not have a choice,
Do as you are told,
The government's voice,

Stay in, go out
We didn't know what to do,
The guidelines kept changing,
Information came from so many views,

We got to a point,
We had had enough,
Look after your own,
So we can get through,

I doubt very much,
Covid will go away,
So we have to learn to live with it,
Until the cure is underway.

NHS

They have never gone unnoticed,
They have always done us proud,
But it took a pandemic,
For us to sing their praise out loud,

The hours they put in,
Alone should get an award,
Their time lost with loved ones,
We stand and applaud,

The service we expect,
A lack of gratitude on our part,
We roll through their doors,
And expect their magic hands to start,

Not thinking about,
Their blood, sweat and tears,
Only our concern for ourselves,
Not their dreams, hopes and fears,

Maybe covid,
Has shown us a way,
To appreciate the army of legends,
And all that they slay,

Their kind eyes,
Their gentle hands,
They fight their own battles,
Whilst dealing with our demands,

A raise in pay,
That's the least they can do,
The NHS held us together,
Through the pandemic we stuck like glue

Regular

When we first met,
It was the usual spill,
But you saw through it,
You knew I was real,

More than the dance,
It wasn't a one-way thing,
More than the money,
Our friendship begins,

We'd talk about me,
And my past,
You were my shoulder to cry on,
Our conversation was vast,

We'd talk about you,
And how you lost your wife,
How cruel the world can be,
How it can cut like a knife,

Engrossed in chat,
I'd miss my call for the stage,
I'd get fined
But you were my guaranteed wage,

You would return again,
And my bills would be paid,
Abundance rained on me,
Every time you stayed,

Regulars come and go,
I knew it wouldn't last forever,
But you were my security,
You lifted my pressure,

Much older and wiser,
You taught me so much,
Business and life
No subject untouched,

The time was here,
To say our goodbyes
We knew this would happen,
Both sad, we couldn't deny,

We helped each other,
In very different ways,
Wise old businessman,
I will forever sing your praise.

Portuguese/Paddy

Born and bred in England,
This much is true,
But I'm Portuguese/paddy,
Many don't have a clue,

My dad was from Madeira,
And my mum's side Irish,
A combination I'm proud,
Something quite conspiring,

My character doesn't go unnoticed
I wear it with pride
A result of both islands combined
I'm loud, proud and very kind

Portuguese are loud and expressive,
Sometimes I'm too much to take
Some find me overpowering
Portuguese/paddy they don't shake

Blessed with my dad's skin
And my mum's sense of humour
I'm forever golden brown
The first to laugh at a rumour

Both places I've visited
Many times
Ireland is so rural
Maderia is a beautiful design

Many more times I will revisit
This I am sure
To show my children their roots
And the places I was born to adore

Friends

We start by wanting many,
Too many is a great deal,
But as we get older,
Our true friends reveal

,
It's always hard losing them,
The ones along the way,
The ones we thought we would have forever,
The ones we thought would never betray,

They show their true colours,
They couldn't conceal over time,
You opened your eyes,
And they are guilty of many crimes,

I like to think,
They get removed for a reason,
You are on to better things,
It's the end of your friendship season,

Though it's hard,
The feeling of loss,
I assure you, it will pass,
You have many bridges to cross,

On the paths,
You choose to take,
Many more friend encounters,
You will make,

Some stay forever,
Others will pass,
Choose your friends wisely,
If it's a friendship you want to last,

Choose someone who brings you joy,
And brings out the best in you,
That you belly-laugh with,
Happiness you both pursue,

The kind of friendship,
Where you feel secure,
Blessed in their company,
Good times assured,

Whoever you choose,
To be in your tribe,
May they always have your back,
And be on a prosperous vibe

Casing

When will people realise,
We are made up of energy,
Our outer casing,
Is just a body full of memories,

The colour of your casing
Means nothing but that,
It holds you all together,
And that is the only fact,

It doesn't matter what colour your case is,
Or what country it was made,
We are all the same inside,
And human courtesy should be displayed,

So many are not like this,
They judge you on your case,
So many small-minded,
A disgrace to the human race,

Those sorts of people,
Their energy is low,
They don't have a high frequency,
So let your vibration show,

Be the bigger person,
And let their judgement ricochet,
Hold your head high,
And be prepared to walk away,

You will meet so many,
As so many fools share our planet,
Smile in their face,
Let that become your habit,

Don't let their words hurt you,
Because that's all they have got,
Your casing is beautiful
Let that never be forgot.

Boxsets

They can keep you up all night,
Or lose hours during the day
Fixated by it,
Too engrossed, you obey,

Whatever your choice is,
YouTube, Netflix or sky,
It will capture you for hours,
And wave your day goodbye,

There's nothing quite like it,
A boxset binge,
Favourite blanket on the sofa,
Your mind tries to infringe,

Lost in the motion,
You are not about to give the right,
To reconnect with the characters,
It is your favourite sight,

Nearing the end,
You start to feel sad,
Knowing you going to lose
All the connections you had,

Boxset blues
Can really hurt,
So fill up your playlist,
And be ready to reassert.

Unknown

You spread through the world,
Like a tornado on speed,
Destroying lives,
Leaving many in need,

You came out of nowhere,
Or so we are told,
Not knowing who to believe,
Many lies we were sold,

We trust the government
Less and less,
Who feed us these lies,
And leave us in distress,

Don't panic do panic,
Like soldiers we conform,
Puppets on a string,
We are made to perform,

Believe what you wish,
It's no one's life but your own,
Man made or not,
It's still very unknown

Deported

Booked a trip to Canada,
Skiing, first time for me,
You didn't want me to go,
You made that clear to see,

So you took it upon yourself
And sprinkled some of your stash,
I had no clue what I was walking into,
I was heading for a car crash,

Stopped at the airport,
Questioned, cuffed and searched,
Off to get their rubber gloves,
On the end of the bench I perched,

You never cease to amaze,
The lengths you willing to go,
Did you want me to get nicked?
Or was that all for show?

I had to count my blessings,
Your efforts were poor,
Twenty-six hours later,
I was knocking on your door,

You got what you wanted
To always be in control,
I'm no longer that character,
I no longer play the role

Perly Spencer

At the height of my bereavement,
There you stood,
Beautiful and majestic,
Slightly misunderstood,

Fresh from the track,
An eager glint in your eye,
You wanted to please,
I was preparing to fly,

Much more than a horse,
More like a friend,
You put a smile on me daily,
Right up until the end,

Upon your back,
My pain you would take,
You put me at ease,
All my troubles you would shake,

Your gentleness amazed me,
Until I sat in your seat,
It all came flooding back,
And you wanted to compete,

That didn't scare me,
Because we are at one,
Nostrils flaring,
To us, this is fun,

The time you gave,
To me was priceless,
Without you, Spencer,
I would have been lifeless,

Animals are much more,
Then we really think,
Unpaid therapist,
They are our missing link.

House of Evilness

The arrival is never soba,
Intoxicated and carefree,
Not thinking of the aftermath,
Just party like it's jubilee,

Greeted with smiles,
And a big welcoming hug,
You step over the threshold,
And all your worries unplug,

The sound of laughter,
Is carried through the walls,
Can't help getting involved,
You ignore all your calls,

Fun is an understatement,
You don't want the night to end,
Everybody is on the same level,
Wanting the party to extend,

But before you know it,
The sun is on the rise,
It is time to go now,
The light is hurting your eyes,

The house of evilness,
Spits out its victims one by one,
Bundling into cabs,
Your body is telling you, you are done,

You promise yourself,
You will never return,
House of evilness hangover,
When will you learn,

You are there next week,
Repeating it once more,
You just can't help yourself,
House of evilness, you can't ignore.

Why Bother

It is so hard to explain,
It wasn't part of the plan,
But here they are,
In the past I ran,

You try hard to bond,
They are nothing like your own,
Very cold people,
The cold shoulder you are shown,

Again and again,
I go against their grain,
Is it actually worthwhile?
The hard façade to maintain,

Time is precious,
And it's my time I invest,
At the end of my tether,
This is shocking at best,

I realise my strengths,
At these tiresome times,
I've done an amazing job
There's a default in your design,

The aftermath of your poor efforts,
Spill onto my life,
It isn't my responsibility,
Your mindlessness leaves me strife,

A big step back,
In which I take,
No point trying to rectify,
This is your mistake,

I have many friends,
That stretch the globe wide,
So unfiltered and fun,
Parent duties they always provide,

You leave me no choice,
But judge you on your faults,
I find you exhausting,
Your array of assault.

Summer

I'm filled full of excitement,
When I know it's approaching,
Those long hot days,
That make you feel like you're floating,

It's truly amazing,
How the big burning ball in the sky,
Releases your serotonin,
And waves winter blues goodbye,

Summer is a big dose of happiness,
Wrapped in laughter and fun,
Making beautiful memories,
Whilst you get kissed by the sun,

Sitting in the park,
Or down the pub with friends,
Feeling of nostalgia,
The sun highly recommends,

It's on a timeline,
So base yourself in its glory,
Worship its rays,
Make the best summer story,

Before you know it,
The yellow face will depart,
You are faced with winter,
And the season cycle restart.

Cheat

A fool you must see,
For this I am sure,
Clandestine and deceitful,
Why did I expect anything more?

You led me up a path,
Of fantasy and delight,
I was naïve and willing,
You made it seem all right,

The sugar coat you wore,
Slowly began to crack,
My instincts were heightened,
All I saw was black,

Reined in my emotions
Before they took hold,
Recentred myself,
For this I am bold,

To whom that hurt me,
Betrayed my trust,
My front seat is booked,
On the inevitable karma bus.

St. Augustine's

A secret institution,
Surely our parents didn't know,
When sending us off,
To the St. Augustine's freak show

A primary school,
I thought would be fun,
Brainwashed by the Bible,
Are how most days begun,

Off to assembly,
We would start with a hymn,
Reciting like robots,
Augustine's characters in Simms,

Young and impressionable,
Once we had permission to sit,
We'd all conform nicely,
With our ears, we'd commit,

My attention wandered,
It didn't take long for me,
To lose complete interest,
Felt like every lesson was R.E,

Permission needed for everything,
Toilet breaks were a no-go,
Unless you like sandpaper,
To wipe down below,

Countless outings,
To the church,
World weary,
On the pews we would perch,

Listen to Father O'Brian,
Mumble on,
Wondering when it's home time,
Wondering how long,

Boredom at it's height,
Most would not dare misbehave,
Fear of Mr. Roland,
Bible in hand he'd enslave,

Out with his guitar,
Songs of praise he would sing,
Holy water in hand,
Banishing our sins,

The Lord is our saviour,
The Lord is king,
Time was on pause,
As he would sing,

Home time,
Couldn't come quick enough,
Another day brainwashed,
Who knew primary was this tough

Witch

When we first met,
I went out of my way,
The best version of me,
I wished to portray,

I bent over backwards,
To make you see,
How happy your son is,
But this you foresee,

Your fabricated opinion,
Your mind was made up,
I was the she-devil's,
Fake boobs, too much makeup,

Born and bred in England,
How dare I?
Should been born in Turkey,
This why,

Your mind is so deluded,
Pathetic and small,
There's no point keep trying,
I'd get more sense from the wall,

The distance you created,
Suits me just fine,
No contact with the witch,
Time to toast, pass me the wine.

The Sea

The vast space it engulfs,
Oceanic of pure mysteries,
So many have explorer it,
To try uncover it's histories,

It's immensity has depth,
Too much for one to comprehend,
The drivers keep on diving,
But they will never reach the end
,
It's mother nature's greatest force,
And she will do as she please,
It may look still and quiet,
While she lures you in with ease,

What lies beneath the surface,
Is anyone's guess,
It's far too big and powerful,
With all the creatures it possesses,

Creatures not yet discovered,
And some from prehistoric times,
All roam their territory freely,
Committing their sea crimes,

I'm so amazed by it,
Call it intrigue or fear,
Educate myself with documentaries,
Hoping my phobia would disappear,

It started when I was young,
Too young to watch *Jaws*,
Fascinated by its rage
But the sea I now withdraw,

Three foot is my max,
I dare not go any farther,
My nerves are on the edge,
As I stand and watch the surfer,

There is no other option,
But to treat it with respect,
Because we are nothing without it,
No sea and the land would disconnect.

Camden

Camden Palace,
You were much more than an event,
Every Friday night,
In my teenage years I spent,

From the pub to train,
And the train to you,
We'd reach for the lasers,
Me and my crew,

Dressed in Adidas three-stripe,
Reebok classics on our feet,
We dance till daylight,
Every Friday we would repeat,

Self-medication,
Bought off a stranger in the line,
Carefree and young,
Drugs we wouldn't decline,

Lost in the music,
Our bodies lose control,
Living for the baseline,
That enters the soul,

The flush of happiness,
That fills the room,
Never wanting it to end,
But the end does loom,

Not to worry,
We will be back next week,
To lift our troubles,
With the music you speak.

Party Peach

Everybody needs that release,
Something to look forward and enjoy,
That's where my alter ego kicks in,
Party Peach I must employ,

She's more than a handful,
She's full of energy and fun,
She becomes louder by the drink,
And won't stop till she's done,

The party is never started,
Before she arrives,
The entrance is powerful,
She sprinkles happiness on people's lives,

She's only got one aim,
To make joyful memories with you,
So let her do her thing,
She will wash away your blues,

That's not to say she's too much,
Some can't handle her shine,
So stay away from her,
If Party Peach is on the wine,

But if you want a good time,
Party Peach is the only way,
It will be eventful,
I promise you will never forget the day.